In telling m,
conversation, and lived experience as I remember
them—not as perfect transcripts, but as emotional
truths. Some names and identifying details have
been changed to protect privacy. What I share
here comes solely from my own experiences
and the lessons I gathered along the way, offered
humbly and without claiming expertise.

This book includes depictions of domestic
violence, sexual abuse, addiction, and mental
illness. I share these experiences not to
shock, but to illuminate patterns that often
remain hidden behind closed doors.

If you are living in an abusive situation,
please know this: abuse is not your fault, and
help does not require perfection or bravery—
only one small step at a time. Leaving abuse
is rarely a single moment; it is a process that
often unfolds quietly and strategically.

Practical guidance for escaping abuse:

If you can, tell one safe person—a friend, coworker,
faith leader, or neighbor—what is happening.
Begin a private safety plan: hide copies
of IDs, birth certificates, medications,
and a small amount of cash.
Keep a record of incidents when it is safe to do so—
dates, injuries, witnesses. This can matter later.
If children are involved, know that courts
often misunderstand abuse dynamics. Seeking
legal guidance early can be protective.
Trust your instincts. Fear is information.

Mental health and crisis resources (U.S.):

988 Suicide & Crisis Lifeline —
Call or text 988 (24/7)
National Domestic Violence Hotline —
1-800-799-SAFE (7233) or thehotline.org
National Sexual Assault Hotline (RAINN)
— 1-800-656-HOPE (4673)
If you are outside the U.S., local resources
can be found at findahelpline.com

If you are not in immediate danger but are carrying
invisible wounds—depression, anxiety, trauma,
or shame—please seek professional care. Therapy,
medication, faith, community, and rest are not
signs of weakness; they are acts of survival.

This story does not offer easy answers. What it offers is companionship. If these pages help even one reader feel less alone, less broken, or more willing to reach for help, then sharing this life has been worth it.

To my son,
and Your sons.

To my daughter,
and Your daughters.

CHAPTER 1- THE GRIND

It doesn't beat steady for pain anymore. Feel like my heart is inching out through my mouth as I yell "Inez" to my neighbor in the apartment below, but she doesn't answer. We go another round, and I know by now I can't win. This time, Walter lands his fist on my left temple, and things go black. Sometime later, I wake to the sound of my baby crying in his crib. My head is pounding like a sandbag just struck it, and I know my ribs have got to be broken. Every breath causes a sharp pain on my right side, and it's almost incapacitating just to move. I lay there bracing myself and collecting the will to get up. Placing my elbow underneath me, I turn and slowly pull myself up from the cold wood floor with my shirt barely there, and I focus on quieting my baby. As I move past the hallway mirror, I see that my left eye is black, and my top lip has a gash in it. I feel ugly - ugly like that dog my 5th-grade classmate had called me. Inis was a popular 5th grader, and he was my first encounter with public humiliation. He said my face looks just like a dog's. At recess, he would bark at me in front of the other children. He made me hate school because I felt like a misfit. I tried my best to fit in. I wanted to be anybody but myself. I often daydreamed of being pretty and popular and coming across him with a strong, tall, and loving male who would wipe the floor with Inis while I stood there in my glory. Back at that time, we didn't know it to be bullying as they call it today, so I just stood there and took it. He taught me right then how to cower and how to curve my eyes down to avoid being noticed. I had an invisible shell that I could go into and be saved from the hurt. I told myself that I was lucky Walter wanted to be with me. When I reached for my baby from the crib, he looked at my face as if he didn't know me. I mumbled his name and twisted a curl in his hair as I always did. He smiled and blurted "mama". I wondered whether this is all I'm destined for in life? Is this what's meant for me? Why wouldn't it be?

It was the spring of 1990, and all people were talking about was how a man named Buster Douglas had knocked out the champion Mike Tyson in round ten or how a man named Nelson Mandela had just been released from imprisonment for fighting South African Apartheid. I wasn't into politics or sports like that, but I knew the guys liked it a lot, so I made myself watch a little here and there. Whenever I would see Tyson in the ring, I swore he was part animal. If it wasn't his tiny, sharp teeth, then maybe it was his squeaky voice; either way, he just wasn't normal to me. As far as athletics go, I could take it or leave it. I was more into fitting in at the time. I would get those Lee press-on nails and whatever hair relaxer was on sale just so I could fit in with the other girls my age. Unlike them, I was thin, pale, and shapeless. They had hips, boobs, and pretty skin.

That same summer, while walking home from White Castles eating a burger, I bumped into a tall, yellow man named Clark. He seemed to have it together; I mean, he was together in a way no man in my family ever was. He spoke well and came from a hardworking middle-class family. They went to college and had nice cars, and family vacations. They even had one of them silver bullet trailers for vacationing in the woods. I didn't mind the 10-year age difference; I felt like he was going to take me places I couldn't go otherwise.

His mother was divorced like mine, but she was really classy and educated. She had a house with a fireplace, and she even owned a restaurant at one time or another. His dad was some kind of real estate executive out in California who made time to play golf. They had much more than we ever dreamed a family could have. They only had two kids, Clark and his younger sister April, who was away to an Ivy

League college at the time. Clark was working at a blueprint company, making decent money and had a really nice car, but he still lived at home with his mom. He and I became really close, and I liked all the new things I learned and saw just being around him and his family. He even helped me get my very first job working at the blueprint company he worked for. It was a one-story building on Clinton Avenue in Irvington. Scruffy part of town, but nothing I wasn't used to.

I didn't know much about sepia or vellum blueprints at the time. Hell, I never even knew anyone who was an architect or engineer, at least not professionally with a degree and all. It was different being around all these folks who didn't look like me at such a young age. I used to spend my breaks talking with the receptionist, who was also African American. Her name was Sheila, and she was round and dark skinned with broken and over-processed hair. Her skin was very smooth, though, and she dressed every day as if she were going off to Sunday school. She was always bragging about what she was doing with the church she went to, and how much shopping she had done that weekend. I could just tell that Sheila never wanted anything more than what she was doing right then and there -answering the boss's phone and highlighting her bible. Maybe she thought I was thinking too highly of myself.

A few months into my job, I decided to go back to

school for my GED. I was surrounded by different people now. I finished the program in no time, and it gave me a boost of confidence when I was on the job. I wanted to fit in at work. The blueprint company was paying me pretty well for my lack any experience, and raises were pretty regular there. I did data entry and scheduled pick-ups to start off. I learned to talk to the engineering firms and architects to schedule their work. The drivers were welcoming when I gave them an assigned drop-off or pick-up. The Bartows had owned this company for years, and it's always been right there on Clinton Avenue in Irvington, New Jersey. They opened a satellite location later on inside Newark's Gateway Center.

I remember every payday we would order fried shrimp platters from a juke joint across the street, and the owners would always order French Onion soup, which I had never heard of. Further up the street was my Aunt Allie, whom I would visit. She was one of my mom's sisters, born the same day as my mom but a few years later. She wasn't the biggest on house cleaning, but she made you feel right at home. You would sit where you could when you were there. She was a waitress at one time, and she would bring home the best fried chicken from Denny's. She met and married a school teacher and became a stay-at-home mom. Shortly after her marriage to Billy, she got cancer. We lost her to breast cancer when she was just forty-six years old.

I swear we didn't know anything 'bout breast cancer til she got it. It was scary, and I don't think she knew what she was up against. No more than two years after she was diagnosed we lost her. Fate would have it that my mom would get it, too. I'll never forget her calling me at work to break the news. My mom is a fighter, though, and she was never one to wallow in her sadness. After the initial shock and sorrow, she went to war on cancer. If her doctor said chemotherapy, she said, " I'm ready". If he said radiation, she replied, "When?" She said she'd be in the shower and chunks of hair would slide out of her scalp. Kicking and fighting her way through all that weakness, hair loss, and sickness, her will remained strong. She was given a clean bill of health twelve months later. Gradually, her strength and hair began to return, and so did her weight. Clark and I were going by regularly to check on her. Often stopping by Cooper's Deli in Newark for a pastrami on rye which has always been my mom's favorite.

One of the most calming and powerful actions you can do to intervene in a stormy world is to stand up and show your soul. Struggling souls catch light from other souls who are fully lit and willing to show it.
-Clarissa Pinkola Estes

Reflection: What part of your soul have you been hesitant to show, and how might revealing it change both you and those around you?

CHAPTER 2- STRAIGHT TO JAIL: DO NOT PASS GO

Clark was never seen as cool by the guys. He was "green" as they would say, and he had a cousin who never had the family Clark had. Charles was a deadbeat, and he never had a car or anything else of his own. Clark, on the other hand, was doing okay but was green, as they would call it on the streets. Turns out his cousin convinced him he could pick up drugs in New York and make big money quickly. Clark wasn't a quick bite, but Charles wore him down over time. It was sunny out, and we both were feeling good about how things were going. Unbeknownst to me, we were doing nothing more than riding over to see the sights in New York. I recall us being pulled over not too long after making a quick stop, where I stayed the car. When the police pulled us over, I didn't think a whole lot of it. I hadn't done anything wrong, and neither had Clark as far as I knew.

The police had him get out of the vehicle and checked him over. There was nothing on him. They didn't physically check me over, but they asked me if I had anything, and I said no. Then they checked the vehicle and sure enough, there was cocaine in the trunk. In no time at all, a tow truck was there to get his white Maxima, and we were hauled off to the Brooklyn House of Detention, a 10-story building on Atlantic Avenue between Brooklyn Heights and Boerum Hill. They held us in jail for two days, and I vowed it would never happen again if they ever released me back to New Jersey.

After processing, I was escorted to a small cell. It was small, cold, and worn. Three other women sat nearby. The youngest one, who was about my age, started talking right away. Asking where I'm from and why I was there. She told me how my Nike boots were gonna be taken by an inmate the minute I was shipped out to Rikers Island. Was she just trying to scare me? I was petrified. I prayed I would stay right there in that holding cell till I was sent home. I heard stories about Rikers Island, and they were never for the faint of heart. It was hardcore. This place had ten separate jails and held thirteen to fourteen thousand inmates on a given day. Rikers is known for jailbreaks, all sorts of brutality, with folks banging on cell bars and yelling. I knew I wouldn't last a day at Rikers Island. By the time lunch came around I didn't want any parts of it. Not that I wasn't hungry, but everything smelled like fish to me, and I just wanted to go home. Besides, what if I had to poop after eating lunch? With everybody sitting around in close quarters watching each other, I don't think so. I prayed harder than I'd ever prayed in my life: God, please, don't let them send me to Rikers. Don't let me disappear in there.

Early the second morning, we went before the judge. I was scared and didn't know what to expect when my name was called. A scrawny white public defender in a bland polyester suit stood at my side. He said he would do all the talking, so I stood there hoping to appear innocent to the presiding judge. How innocent could I have really looked, though, dressed in neon Nike boots, tight blue jeans, gold jewelry, and fingerwaves in my hair. Maybe he thought I was just another hoochie mama making my first debut in the legal system. Regardless of what he thought, I feared for the worst. I had no idea what to expect, so I just stared forward.

The case was called, and the public defender began discussing the charges and how he had reached a deal with the prosecutor based on it being a first offense and all. The judge cut his eyes over at me and then began reviewing something on paper.

The courtroom was full of folks, and sheriffs were standing everywhere just waiting to be needed. Waiting to haul me off to Rikers Island so my boots, my butt, and everything else could be taken, I thought to myself. I felt a sudden anger for Clark. How could he, being ten years older than me, let me get myself in some trouble behind his mess? You could tell Clark was an amateur and didn't know what the hell he was doing either. The charges were dismissed based on our staying out of trouble for a few years. I was so happy I bout hugged the public defender 'cept he leaned off to the side to be sure I wasn't touching his shiny polyester suit. It didn't bother me one bit. They didn't have to worry about ever seeing my narrow ass again, and I mean never. We were released right away, and our personal belongings were returned at the front. We hopped the PATH train headed for New Jersey. It was great to be home. Clark vowed never to mess with drugs again.

I guess you could say I was settling into my adult life by now. Vanity had nothing to do with my relationship with Clark because he was a lanky, high-pitched, but well-spoken man. He was way more mature than I was. He always wore ties and shirts and introduced me to traveling and eating at nice restaurants. Fast food was a splurge for us when I was growing up. This was all new to me. I was in no hurry for him to meet my extended family. But when he did, he was nice about it, never passing any judgment or anything.

A year later, he moved us into our own apartment. It was a two-bedroom apartment on the second floor of a storefront building on Broad Street in Elizabeth, New Jersey. It was a starter apartment, and his family gave us some furniture to start us off. We rode together back and forth to work each day. He was always eager to make us Taylor ham and fried eggs on a roll for breakfast. He liked the idea of having a family. The days quickly turned into weeks and the weeks into months. Before long, I got pregnant with my daughter, Ava. This was the happiest he'd ever been, so I knew Clark would want to get married. We held off the discussion until she was born.

I remember hearing Clark approaching our apartment door after work, and I ran to the door to unlock it. Running to the door at eight months pregnant was not a good idea. Water gushed down the inside of my thighs. We knew it was time to go. After two days in the hospital and no contractions, they induced my labor. Everything seemed to speed up at that point, and before I knew it, Dr. Human was saying push and bracing himself for a catch. My daughter shot out with enough speed that Dr Hyman caught her like a football. He was bent at the waist and caught her with his arms in a circle. I gave birth to our daughter that January; the year we had the "Storm of The Century". Snow was everywhere.

We had a fire-engine red Ford Bronco, and we were able to go anywhere in that thing. It had a few rust spots, but it was tough as nails, and besides, we had saved up to pay for that truck outright. Clark was good at saving.

That winter, places in New York got forty-something inches of snow, and with us being only 45 minutes outside of New York, I thought the snow would never stop falling. Ice cycles hung everywhere, some as long as two feet, so I was extra careful when walking under a roof ledge. It brought back memories of a girl where I grew up who had an ice cycle lodged in the back of her head. You never forget the sight of that; a bloody mess all over Tina's blond hair. It was very disturbing to see, but somehow she recovered.

We were shut in a lot that winter, but inside the apartment, with my baby in my arms and Clark by my side, it felt like the beginning of a new life. The winter sped by, and I was mighty happy to see the spring come. I turned twenty that year, and Clark and I went to Vegas and literally jumped the broom in a roadside chapel. Wearing a cheap white satin dress with my baby girl in my arms, Clark and I exchanged vows. An Elvis impersonator led the wedding service, which was no more than fifteen minutes long. We spent the rest of our time in Vegas eating at five-dollar buffets and enjoying the sunshine. When we came home, we jumped right back into our routine of working, cooking, and changing diapers as if nothing had ever happened.

You break the rules, and you become the hero. I do it, and I become the enemy.
-Wanda to Dr Strange in Marvel's Dr. Strange In The Multiverse of Madness.
Reflection: When have you followed the same rule as someone else, yet be judged differently and how did that shape the way you see yourself?

CHAPTER 3-INTO THE ABYSS

I was ready to learn to drive. I wanted more independence. Clark taught me to drive in that red Bronco. We would go across the street to the A&P parking lot, and I would get behind the wheel. At first, my braking was so heavy that it would always lurch us forward when the vehicle stopped. He moved me out onto the roadways to drive, and in no time, I was able to get my driver's license. Once I was able to get my driver's license, I bought my first car. It was a second-hand blue Hyundai Excel. I was proud of that accomplishment. Having a car and a driver's license was not something most of the people did where I grew up, so it felt good that I could do this. I didn't want to fit in anymore or be like everyone else.

Our daughter was growing in leaps and bounds by

now. She was so smart. At three years old, I enrolled her in a private Pre-K class, and she's excelled academically ever since. We didn't allow a TV in our home until she was in 2nd grade. It was a good time to think about buying a house with a yard for her to play in. Clark's credit wasn't the best, so my mom co-signed my loan so we could have a home. It was a light green house with two bedrooms and a garage in Roselle, New Jersey. It was a fixer-upper, but it was ours, and it gave our daughter a place to play and make friends. By the third year of marriage, I was restless. I separated from Clark and began seeing other people. One night, I brought home a guy named Ben. Ben was a Morganhouse student working in New Jersey for the summer. Ben sat on the couch while I went to the bedroom to hang my coat up. When I opened my bedroom door, Clark was sitting in there waiting with the lights out. When I saw him there, I panicked. I told Ben to run, and he did. He ran out through the front door and out into the night. I never saw that punk again, thank God, but it was too late for Clark and me. The age difference was just too much for me. He still came around from time to time to spend time with our daughter.

I can't say for sure when it began, but he started using drugs, and he was not trying to hide it. He would cook it up in spoons with a lighter and leave traces lying around. He was selling everything by now to support his habit. I will always recall him crying to me like a baby, standing there in the snow outside my house in Roselle with a television in his hands to sell for drugs. He said it had control over him, and he didn't know if he could ever be free. I felt helpless. Angry. And alone. I thought 'bout how on the news tonight Princess Di got twenty-six million this week in her divorce from Prince Charles, and here people like me and Clark can't even live, never mind living large. Right then, I knew this would leave me to parent our daughter solo, and so I did. His mom would help with babysitting and even shopping to provide for her, so it made things easier. I got promoted at work, and that too was a big help.

Our daughter was my world, and I knew I would never let anyone harm her. She was so carefree in a way I never was. I was always afraid of what men do to little girls like her. Molestation was no stranger when and where I grew up. When I was seven, my uncle Sully, a tall man with a big stomach and a gentle face, lifted me and placed me over my grandma's couch. I was lying face down with my feet dangling over the back of the couch. Then he pulled my panties aside and rubbed his penis around my vagina. He never inserted it for fear of tearing me or leaving behind evidence. I did not understand sex or rape. No one had ever sat me down and said anything about that sort of thing. I felt paralyzed, not knowing what to do about what was happening. I had never seen it on television or anywhere. It was at this time that I learned the family's lessons:

-Endure what hurts
-Don't speak what shames
-And whatever you do, keep moving like nothing happened

This continued until we moved away when my mama remarried after leaving my dad. Later, when I would see Uncle Sully, he always looked sorry. Sorry or not, I was sure to never let myself be alone around him ever again. In time, I learned more about sex and that rape is wrong. I learned that incest was a sin. I wondered what my grandmother would say if she knew her son had done that to me. What would my mom do? Would anybody believe me? Maybe they would be so ashamed of me that everything would fall apart and I would be to blame. I stored it away in that invisible shell that Inis, the 5th grader, introduced me to. To this day, my uncle Sully never married or had a real family of his own. They say God knows best.

The men in my family weren't strangers to violence either. My own dad used to beat my mom until she finally left him. I remember one of my uncles stabbing his wife in the butt right through her jeans because she was out when he got home. They had a little apartment on Market Street in Passaic, New Jersey. We were all out for the day because it was nice outside, and she hadn't made him dinner when he got home. He grabbed a pair of heavy iron scissors and stabbed her right in the butt, right through her jeans. She didn't go to the hospital, not even for a tetanus shot, because she didn't want him to get in trouble. She forgave him; she always did. That's what I saw: women forgiving, enduring, surviving.

When we have a desire to have a thing or experience, the first images of the desire are pure.
-Iyanla Vanzant; In The Meantime
Reflection: Which of your desires felt innocent at the beginning, and at what moment did omplexity or compromise enter the picture?

CHAPTER 4- FINDING MY WAY

F ew of my aunts and uncles were married, but they all had at least one child. Together, my mom and dad had two children, and I was the youngest. Even among the females in my family, there were wounds. I was a very light-skinned child in contrast to family members of my age, and they would pick at me by calling me high-yellow or white girl. They teased me like it was a joke, like it was love. At first, I just assumed it was how families in the south had fun with each other, but words leave marks, too. Sometimes sharper than fists. It made me strong in some ways, but it also taught me how to disappear inside myself, how to carry secrets like stones in my chest. Stones that would grow heavier with every year. I don't think we ever outgrew putting each other down – to this day, it's not uncommon among females to be greeted with "girl, you're putting on some weight" or "why don't you have a husband yet" instead of a loving hello. My sister Clem has always been the quiet type. She was the mother hen of the bunch, so reserved. Growing up, she would do her best to keep me out of trouble.

When I was growing up, I never gave much thought to becoming a mom someday and raising my own children. Before there was ever my daughter Ava or my son Jay, there were babies never seen, babies I never mothered. When Clark first got me pregnant at eighteen, I didn't tell him. I didn't tell anyone. I was embarrassed. At that time, black women were gossiped about for having babies while unmarried. I caught the bus to a clinic in South Orange, New Jersey, and had an abortion. I remember this place was so cold, dimly lit, and full of silence. No one smiled. My young mind was busy visualizing what an embryo might look like, whether they could hear, and could move. I wondered whether I would be hurting afterwards. When they called me in, I undressed and lay back on a small table with my feet in stirrups. The doctor went through a list of potential risks, including hemorrhaging. They asked me some questions about my general health and gave me a shot of something. Things became a blur very quickly, and when I awoke, I was in a small recovery area wearing a maxi pad the size of a dish towel.

The nurse told me that when I was ready, I could

sit up, get dressed, and leave. Just like that. I felt weird lying there. I uncurled myself on the little cot and began to dress. I peeled my panties forward to see the maxi pad they put there while I was still under anesthesia. It was dry as a bone. Maybe the baby was too little to even have veins and blood, or so I had hoped. I wasn't hurting, so I didn't bother calling a cab. She gave me some final instructions, and I walked out the front door and off to the bus stop like nothing had happened. But something had happened. I carried the silence like a scar no one could see. Feelings of guilt about what had just happened started to set in, but I just stared out the window of the bus, trying to distract my thoughts as much as possible. I prayed for forgiveness. I slept for a day or two after that and I didn't have much to say to Clark either. I ignored his calls for a good week. I didn't want to be near a man at that time.

I got myself on birth control pills before Clark, and I was intimate again. He was never one to ask many questions. Maybe he didn't think much of it. A year went by, and I started letting my guard down with my birth control pills. I would skip here and there, but I think it was mostly because I wasn't worried about becoming a mom. When Clark got me pregnant the second time, I was ready. Ready for the journey of motherhood. I had my baby girl, Ava. She was perfect: bald, plump, caramel-skinned, and with the cutest dimples. She was a happy baby.

When someone shows you who they are, believe them the first time.
-Maya Angelou
Reflection: When have you ignored or explained away who someone showed themselves to be--and what did it ultimately cost you?

CHAPTER 5-LOOK BOTH WAYS

There's a five-year gap between my son and daughter. When I got pregnant with my son, Jay, my life changed. His dad, Walter, didn't think we should become parents. Maybe he didn't want to disappoint his parents with, yet another baby and he still was not married and living at home with them. There was no convincing him to have this baby. I cried the whole way to the abortion clinic as we rode in his brown Jeep Cherokee down the Garden State Parkway. I was so distraught about his willingness to force things to end this way that I actually threatened to leave him. He felt pity and agreed to hear me out. Walter had a baby daughter he was not welcomed to see so he wasn't ready to have another child at this time. We were having unprotected sex, and I got pregnant. It was time to be responsible about our choices, I told him. We both cried, and I was able to go home that evening with my little baby growing inside. We learned that we were going to have a son. Walter was the proudest dad around when the baby was born. It was like night and day from that first conversation.

On the night I went into labor, my water broke, and I decided to remain home a little longer. Turns out that was not a good idea. We rode in that brown Jeep Cherokee to the hospital to give birth. I'll never forget the news blaring from the radio that President Bill Clinton denied sexual relations with his twenty-one-year-old intern, Monica Lewinsky. I lay there in the back seat of that truck, wondering how easily families are destroyed. It was very hard to believe, but not as hard as the next building contraction in my belly. I clenched my fists at my side and began my pursed-lip breathing til we reached the hospital. They met us at the door with a wheelchair, and within fifty minutes of my arrival at the hospital, Jay was born. They laid him on my chest so I could see him. He was light like me, but with hazel eyes and sandy colored hair. He had a red circle in his right eye from pressure when coming through my pelvis, but he was precious nonetheless. He left quite a squirt of meconium on my chest when they lifted him away. His big sister Ava stood by, tickled pink to have a little brother.

When Walter and I first met, things were great, and I know they usually are, but I swear he was different. He was a shy, inexperienced, and very handsome personal trainer at a gym I had joined. He was a marine too. He was a reason for me to go the extra mile when getting ready for the gym each night. I was never into the skimpy biker shorts and all, but I would make sure my sneakers were clean, and my hair was neat before I left the house. We enjoyed talking to one another, and I was careful not to give him too much play. I was gonna be patient. I couldn't risk rushing a thing, I mean, this was the one.

He invited me to his marine ball a few weeks after we met, and things progressed from there. He came from a small family in Maplewood, New Jersey. He was a junior and the only son, to be exact. His dad was a big-time newspaper writer. His mom was a homemaker. He had one sister who was working for a New York book publisher. He started his education at Coppin State University, but dropped out and became a marine. I sensed he was a little immature because he wanted to play video games whenever he wasn't working. He had never lived outside his parents' house, so I had a little more experience than him, but it didn't matter. He was thin but muscular, and he had nice pink lips that he would lick quite often. He was very sexy too.

When he started staying over, he would tiptoe up behind me and bend me over the washing machine while I was doing laundry. He kissed and massaged me from head to toe. He would sex me like a crazed sailor stranded on a deserted island. I was madly in love. He was my first true love. I wanted to try something I heard about with Walter. A friend told me about a sex move that was guaranteed to make you lose your mind. I thought she was crazy, but I wanted to hear more. She went on about how she releases in no time flat due to the pleasure and intensity. The word intensity made me skittish, but I played it off so she could be open about her experience. This act was known as the triple threat for women. She tells me that during the moment when your partner is giving you oral pleasure, he just needs to apply light pressure with one finger against the opening of your vagina and apply pressure with another finger against your anus. With no penetration at all, she said she explodes every time. I thought about it many times, but never did get the courage to tell a man what to do to please me. I was content having a man, plus Walter was good with children. My daughter loved being around him, and so we would take trips together. He was like a big kid to her. The older women in my family all wanted him to date their daughters. He was charming, well-mannered, and handsome.

A year later, I was pregnant, and so he moved in with me. With neither one of us making much money, things began getting tight. I was still living in that two-bedroom house, which I bought from an Amish widow in Roselle, New Jersey. It won't look much to look at, but it was my first. I chose one of those adjustable-rate mortgages that looked good in the beginning but quickly became more than I could afford. I decided to do a short sale and give my house back to the bank, and move to an apartment where we could both start fresh. He was all for it.

One can only face in others what one can face in oneself.
-James Baldwin; Nobody Knows My Name
What parts of yourself have you struggled to face, and how has that shaped the way you respond to those same traits in others?

CHAPTER 6-
DETOUR AHEAD

We moved away to Philadelphia to get a fresh start. We picked a roomy two-bedroom apartment near Fairmont Park on the ninth floor with a view of the city skyline. The building had everything from a hair salon, playground, restaurants, shops, and a swimming pool. It was the next best thing to Disney World for a family starting out. We were very excited. I was out of work on maternity leave, but I was getting disability, and Walter had gotten a job with BACCSI, which was a division of Bell Atlantic. We were doing okay. The kids loved Philadelphia, and I was learning my way around.

My mom came out to visit one time, and I could tell she was happy for me. She felt like the kids, and I was going to be okay. Walter began spending time at the casino shortly after we moved to Philly. Blackjack was his game of choice. He could easily spend six or seven hours at it. It quickly became a problem. We had our first fight in the hallway right outside our bedroom. He was yelling about how he was a grown man. He poured a vase of dirt in my hair and pushed me into the wall. I dressed the kids, and we left. We found a hotel nearby to spend the night. I was heartbroken.

Our baby was barely two months and everything was coming to an end. The kids slept much soundly than I did that night. I occasionally gazed over at them and was glad they had escaped into a world of peaceful sleep. We went back home the next day, and Walter came in about an hour after us. He was calm. He seemed very happy to see us, and he apologized repeatedly. He ordered three dozen red and pink roses to say he was sorry for losing his temper. I had never been surrounded by so many roses in my life. I believed he was sorry, but I was still scared of him. I remember how my dad used to beat my mom, and she found it in her heart to forgive him, but she didn't stay with him long. She left him, and we moved away.

I was hoping Walter and I could be a family and that the abuse I had seen as a child would stay in my past. As time went on, it started up again. He just wasn't gonna stop gambling or lying, and God knows what else, and the minute I said something about it, he would haul off and pop me side of the face. I knew if we were going to beat this, we had to move away from any casinos. I found myself a job in Jersey City, New Jersey, so we ended up moving back to New Jersey. He was able to keep his job with BACCSI, which was now Verizon. His parents were able to help out with the kids when they were working. The gambling eventually gave way to another addiction: women. It started, I suspect, over the computer. This was when AOL announced your messages with "you've got mail". I would here this all evening when he came home. He became more blatant with it, and the fights got even worse.

I tried not to get him angry, but keeping quiet while he ran around was harder than I thought. Coming home from Brother's BBQ with dinner in hand I began to get a sinking feeling in the pit of my stomach. Suddenly I already know that today just isn't my day. When I reach our apartment I approach him about my concerns, and when he blows them off, I push his PlayStation to the floor to get his attention. Wrong move. He grabs me by the hair as hard as he can, bringing me down to the floor. I yell for help.

Feel like my heart is inching out through my mouth as I yell "Inez" to my neighbor in the apartment below, but she doesn't answer. We go another round, and I know by now I can't win. This time, Walter lands his fist on my left temple, and things go black. Sometime later, I wake to the sound of my baby crying in his crib. My head is pounding like a sandbag just struck it, and I know my ribs have got to be broken. Every breath causes a sharp pain on my right side, and it's almost incapacitating just to move. I lay there bracing myself and collecting the will to get up. Placing my elbow underneath me, I turn and slowly pull myself up from the cold wood floor with my shirt barely there, and I focus on quieting my baby. As I move past the hallway mirror, I see that my left eye is black, and my top lip has a gash in it. I feel ugly-ugly like that dog my 5th-grade classmate called me.

When I reached for my baby from the crib, he looked at my face as if he didn't know me. I mumbled his name and twisted a curl in his hair as I always did. He smiled and blurted "mama". By now, I was telling myself I had to stay for the kids to have a decent life with two parents and all. The last thing the world needed was another black single mom with no real career and no man in sight. If I could keep my abuse to myself like I did when I was a little girl, then nobody would get hurt. It was up to me to keep the family together. There was no love anymore; only sex and violence.

Within two years of having our son Walter got me pregnant again. The relationship was so broken that I knew it wasn't the time, and so it was a mutual decision to abort the embryo. I had to kick and scream to keep the first pregnancy, so I knew he didn't want a second one. At that point, I should have left because there was nothing good coming. I stayed, though, and the fights and cheating continued. Sex was the only thing left; it was the only card I had left to play. When I felt lonely or thought he was cheating, I wanted sex and would be waiting when he showed up. With my breast hanging out of a tank top and a thong secured between the slit of my plump ass, my body was throbbing to melt all over him. I would take long baths and rub lotion and perfume all over me before he arrived. During intimacy, I felt I had finally harnessed some control over my chaotic life. A year later, I was pregnant again, but he would never know this time. Tired of the humiliation and disrespect, I finally got the courage and left him the day before I had my final abortion. I asked God's forgiveness for the abortions, and I pictured my babies in heaven bouncing on God's knee.

We can be overloved, underloved, overworked, underworked...each costs much.
-Clarissa Pinkola Estes
Reflection: Which imbalance have you lived with the longest, and how has it shaped the way you give or receive now?

CHAPTER 7-THE RECKONING

I knew I had to accept my role in what was going on in my life. I had to face the demons of my childhood and the convictions of my choices as an adult. I couldn't blame Walter, I couldn't blame my uncle Sully, I couldn't blame Inis the 5th grader, I couldn't blame anyone. Weakened by years of chaos, instability, and little self-awareness, I entered what seemed to be an eternal war of custody with Walter over our son. Walter's dad was a very influential man, and he did not condone me moving away to build a new life with his grandson in tow. I knew they had the finances to get the results they wanted in this case. I was broke with only faith to carry me through this. I joined a church to deepen my faith and to give my life some stability.

Family court does not operate on morality or

memory—it operates on paperwork, resources, and perception. I learned this the hard way. Custody proceedings unfolded in a series of hearings scheduled roughly every sixty days. Each appearance drained time, money, and emotional endurance. Walter's family retained private counsel early, while I relied on limited funds and faith. Court-appointed professionals—evaluators, therapists, and a forensic psychiatrist—were presented as neutral, though their services were paid for by one side.

The psychological evaluation became the axis on which everything turned. Dr. Dasher's report framed "stability" in terms of income, housing, and perceived emotional control, not history of abuse. Bruises fade. Trauma responses remain—and in court, those responses were interpreted as instability rather than injury.

Allegations of domestic violence were treated as "conflict between adults," while my financial hardship was framed as risk. Each continuance felt like a slow erosion of motherhood. Supervised visits were discussed. Relocation was challenged. My voice was measured against credentials, and credentials always carried more weight.

I learned that family court often asks: Who looks calmer? Who sounds credible? Who can pay to keep going?

Not: Who was harmed?

By the time the final order was entered, the outcome felt less like a judgment and more like attrition.We were in court every other month for two years. Dr. Dasher was the "hired gun" psychiatrist who deemed Walter a better fit to provide for our son. Every chance Walter got to be alone with our son, he filled his head with the worst someone could say to a child about his mom. In the meantime, I saved by putting away every penny for our move to Virginia.

One afternoon while I was at work I met Elmore. His company provided services for the firm I worked for at the time. Elmore is a short caramel-colored guy that wore glasses and a baseball cap. He had nice teeth; in fact, it's one of the first things you notice. He was not ideal when it came to looks, but God knows I needed something different in my life. Looks or hot sex on a platter was not going to cut it this time. I was done trying to fit in. I was done with the drama. It was take me as I am from here on. Our first date was at a restaurant called Bice's in West Orange, New Jersey. It was a nice evening, and we followed up with calls to each other a few times a week. I slowly started meeting each other's families, and for our first Valentine's Day, I scheduled a private dance lesson for us at a dance school nearby. He was blown away; after that, I couldn't beat him off with a stick.

Elmore had never had any kids or been married, and he was thirty-four. I saw this as odd at first. Then I thought this was just what I was looking for: a blessing in disguise. He was in church, he could cook, and had his own little apartment. He even accepted my rules about mandatory STD testing and protection. He was with me when custody started falling apart with my son's dad. He saw firsthand the torment I lived. I was so grateful for his shoulder. When I told him I was moving to Virginia, he didn't argue. I had bought a home in Virginia that I use when I visit family in the area. He was willing to make it work. A year after I moved, he proposed to me, and we set a date to get married. He was still living in New Jersey at the time, but he planned to move to Virginia as soon as his new business was financially stable. I was working at a real estate company at the time, but I knew it wasn't for me. I sat there for hours every day prospecting and taking messages for other agents. I was horrible at selling real estate, so little was coming in.

The custody war with Walter ate all of my savings. I had nothing left. Work wasn't steady, and we used food stamps to make ends meet. I was not above having a TV dinner for lunch or cereal for supper. Times were hard. One night, I lay praying we would survive the cold that night. I had no money for heating oil, and we only had a single electric heater in one room of the house. I piled coats on the blankets we lay under. Hopeful that our body heat would help, I was on one side of the bed with my daughter on the other and my baby son in the middle. We huddled around him since he was too thin to withstand the cold. I made it look like we were camping in a tent. God heard my prayers, and we survived like we always did.

When the smoke settled in the custody battle, I lost. A mother's love knows no boundaries. Even when we are ill-equipped to provide for our offspring, we spend our last breath fighting to the end. It will always mark the saddest day of my life, the day my brother-in-law came to retrieve my seven-year-old to give to Walter. I walked with him to the car with his bags and hugged his little shoulders as if there was no tomorrow. He was so innocent, standing there with his Spiderman gloves on. My face immediately turned hot, and the tears refused to wait until I had turned my back on my son. He couldn't understand. I was crushed. A child I birthed and cared for was yanked from me. When I reached the house, my body was shaking, and I simply collapsed face down on my bed, where I stayed for days, overcome with disbelief and sadness.

Start where you are. Use what you have. Do what you can.
-Arthur Ashe
Reflection: What is one small step you can take today using exactly what you have, right where you

are?

CHAPTER 8- SECONDS ANYONE

L ater that Spring, I went back to college to take some basic courses toward my nursing degree. It helped to take my mind off all the things that went wrong in the custody case. Things were going as planned with our wedding date set for May 29th. Elmore and I got married, and it was beautiful. I planned and arranged everything about that wedding in one year. I always had a creative mind, and with me growing up having very little, I knew how to be resourceful. I helped decorate everything except the cake.

The wedding was outdoors, lakeside at a country club in the country. I hired a violinist to play "If It

Wasn't For Your Love" by Heather Hedley. When I walked down the aisle, there were rose petals under my feet and my dad at my side. I was surprised that he actually was there for me on my wedding day. I was a princess. His family and mine lit the wedding candles, and everyone just couldn't stop smiling. The reception was inside, in an illuminated ballroom fit for Cinderella. Food and champagne were everywhere. We danced and greeted people for what seemed like an eternity. The party continued later on at our house; I mean, folks were everywhere. The weather was perfect, and I finally felt I belonged to someone. For some reason, I always wanted my last name to change, and so it did. I was now Mrs. Gray. I even got it on my license plate.

We had a short honeymoon on the Outerbanks of North Carolina. It was very romantic. We picnicked at night on the sand and slept in late most mornings. We visited the lighthouses and ate saltwater taffy. It was nice. We had to hurry back because he was the only person running his business, and I had school waiting. Nursing school was proving to be more than I ever imagined. All the sciences and math were taking a toll. I would see classmates crying in agony over a grade that was within points of passing, but unfortunately not close enough. I was happy I had a support system at home. Elmore's business was new, but he was determined to make it work. He was doing pest control for apartment houses and companies, slowly things began to take off.

We tried to do little things here and there between his work and my school to grow our marriage. Being in school and all, I knew I didn't want to chance getting pregnant, so one day I decided to have an IUD inserted, and I didn't tell Elmore. He wanted kids right away, and I wasn't ready. When the bill for my IUD came in the mail, Elmore opened it. He went crazy. I don't know if he blanked out, but he came at me while I was eating a bowl of cereal. Milk went flying one way, and I tried to run the other, but he wouldn't let me. He shoved me onto that off white chaise we had downstairs, and he turned me face down. He took the pillows off the chaise and pressed down as hard as he could on the back of my head with them pillows. I was struggling to slip myself over so I could breathe, but he was sitting on my back. I was mumbling, "Please, please, Elmore, you're killing me". He didn't even budge. I stopped kicking and mumbling and tried to preserve the air left in my lungs. I couldn't be going through this again. What was it about me? I breathed as lightly as I could, sucking air from the fabric underneath me. When he finally got up, my body hit the floor. I was literally on my last breath. I gasped and gasped and gasped for dear life. When I was able to stand, I got to the phone to call 911, but in one swoop, he ripped the phone from the cord and threw it to the floor. I yelled up the stairs to my teenage daughter to call the police. She had a cell phone, and so she did.

When they arrived, his eyes were as big as quarters. He started lying to them about how I made this up, and I was stunned. I had never seen him act this way. There was no denying the evidence. The marks on my face and neck, the lipstick smeared on the chaise. In no time, they took his ass off to jail. That was the closest I've ever come to death, and sadly, it was at my husband's hands. There was a shelter for domestically abused women in Suffolk called the Genieve Shelter. I had never openly talked to anyone about being abused, but something had to change. I couldn't keep dragging this heavy baggage alone. Still scared to tell any of my family about my problems for fear of being judged, I went to this shelter. They gave me the support I needed to keep from dropping the charges against this Elmore. At the hearing, the court took the case under advisement for two years since it was a first offense. If he didn't commit any more crimes, then it would be removed from his record. I was shocked because Virginia is one of the strictest states around when it comes to domestic violence. I thought he should have at least gotten probation. I trusted that this was one of those situations when justice would still come, just not from the courts.

I spent the summer focused on my schooling. I had enrolled in Chemistry at one campus and Biology at another. If I didn't pass those sciences that summer, I couldn't get into the Registered Nurse program

I was applying for until the following year. There was no time to waste; unlike most students, I was already in my thirties, and there was a lot at stake if I didn't do something soon. I took to the books, learning all I could about anions and mitochondria. It was then that I learned how to make little rhymes of information to help me remember things on my tests. If the lab was open that weekend, I was there looking at diagrams and piecing together heart chambers. I had to be creative because passing these courses was not an option. I promised Ava and Jay we would do something when my classes finished, and so we did. We packed our bags and drove to Kings Dominion for a few days. My daughter brought along her best friend, and they had a good time. I rested and read a little, but mostly I chauffeured them around, which was fine with me. When we went home, there were heaps of mail piled up on the front porch. I dug through it, throwing aside anything that wasn't pressing. I came across a letter from the School of Nursing at the college and it read:

Congratulations! On behalf of the School of Nursing I am please to offer you full admission into the Associate of Applied Science (AAS) in Nursing Program at Paul D. Camp Community College for the Spring of 2002.

I had been accepted into the Registered Nurse program. I was ecstatic. I must have said thank you, God, over two hundred times that day.

When our grief cannot be spoken, it falls into the shadow and re-arises in us as symptoms. So many of us are depressed, anxious, and lonely.
-Francis Weller, The Wild Edge of Sorow
Reflection: What would it mean for you to give language to a grief you've kept in the shadows?

CHAPTER 9-THE NEED TO NURSE

In no time at all, the school year was starting. A week or two into the nursing program, I started thinking about how I didn't want to be divorced and how I wanted someone to share the rest of my life with. What good was living your dreams alone? Maybe women my age gave up too fast. Maybe perseverance and sacrifice weren't part of our make-up. Was I really to forgive Elmore? I called Elmore, and initially he didn't take my calls, but days turned to weeks, and he eventually agreed to meet me at a burger joint to talk.

I always knew I was a nurturer. I suppose I could take the brokenest of men and fix them right up. I could love them into loving me. In my man, I was determined to find the dad I never had, the good looks I longed for, and the acceptance that I never felt.

He was on time for once, and so we sat at a booth toward the back of the place out of the way. I told Elmore we couldn't just walk away from something we both worked so hard to get. I told him our love was different. I all but begged for our marriage back. He was slow talking, but he came around. He said he was still angry because I got an IUD without telling him, and then I called the police when he got upset, so now he has a record, and it's all my fault. We moved back in together, and things slowly started thriving again. Both our parents were happy. We began our next family trip, to Jamaica, we said. One night, we lay in bed, and we heard a knock at the door around 11:30 pm. He went to the door, and I noticed when he returned, he was a totally different color. His words couldn't come out right. His breathing was heavy, and his hands couldn't be controlled.

He said someone he met while we were separated found out where we lived and was refusing to give up on what they could have become. He was furious. He called the police to handle the young lady, and they were at the house in no time. She reluctantly left, but I demanded to know everything. What woman shows up at another woman's house at 11:30 at night expecting not to get her ass whipped? I made it clear that the only way we would be a family again is if he let his parents and mine know how he had betrayed his vows. We called them and had several talks; there was prayer, and he cried in guilt and disappointment. We even got the preacher to counsel us about what had happened in the eyes of God. He became a very attentive husband, waiting on me hand and foot. He called me throughout the day to assure me that he was never going to make that mistake twice. We bounced back, and things slowly began to heal. By now, school and life in general were really making a sport of me. I felt stretched and bruised mentally.

Sleep was a rare treat for me. I started snacking on all the wrong things just to stay awake while studying. Clinicals were very trying, and I was burning out fast. A few weeks before my finals, Elmore stayed out all night and didn't take any of my calls. I feared the absolute worst. He was dead or had flipped the car over a bridge and couldn't get out. I even called his parents in New Jersey to see if they knew anything. The following night, around 7:30, I heard the front door open, and he locked it behind him. I met him at the staircase and asked him what had happened. He told me he stayed at his office all night to finish up some new contracts. When I said his car was not parked at his office, he said he hid it behind the building next door so he couldn't be disturbed. I then asked for local receipts of where he had eaten his meals the last thirty-six hours, but he didn't have any. Before I knew it, my hands left my side, and I grabbed him by the collar as tight as I could, leaving a scratch on the left side of his neck. He yelled, "Get off me!" He broke away and ran outside. I went to our bedroom to cool down and put on my slippers. By the time I walked out the front door, I saw police pulling up in front of the house. I almost felt like he had set me up. Was he trying to take my house for himself and some other woman?

This time, the police took me to jail for assaulting him, and the scratch on his neck was all the proof he needed. It never even mattered to the officers that he was out running around on me; they didn't want to hear it, and the cell bars locked behind me. Sitting there in my pajamas and one slipper, all I could do was cry. How could he let his wife be arrested after he had run out on her? Where was his conscience? Was this get get-back for his arrest after choking me? How could he explain this to our families? After processing, I was released with an upcoming court date. Elmore drove me home that night in silence. In my mind, I felt he always wanted to get me back for having him arrested when he smothered me on that chaise. He never did outright accept responsibility for that incident, and he was one to carry a grudge to his grave.

Nothing was ever the same again after that. By the time the NCLEX state boards came around, my marriage was over. The night before my exam, I walked into our bedroom, and Elmore had fallen asleep lying on his back with his shirt off. I noticed a fresh tattoo on his back, which was still raised and unhealed. I bent over to take a closer look, and this fool rose up from his sleep and yelled, "Get away from me". I asked him why I didn't know he was out being tattooed that day when he had told me he was at work. He asked me why I was snooping around him when he was sleeping. I knew right then there was more to that story. He said if I touch his tattoo, he's having me arrested again. I left the room and sat in the spare bedroom in disgust. Here I was with the biggest exam of my life in a few hours, and this fool is lying and sneaking around again. I lay my head down in hopes of getting some sleep before my exam, but no sleep came.

An hour before my alarm was set to go off, I got up and paced the floor a little bit. I made myself some coffee and started getting ready for the day. I did a last-minute check to make sure I had my NCLEX authorization to test letter and my ID. Elmore was going to meet me after the exam so we could ride together to New Jersey for his family reunion. I couldn't think of a worse way anyone could spend the night just before the state board exam. I was a bag of nerves going into the testing area. I sat down at this little desk with a computer and headphones. There was some scrap paper and a pencil on the desk. I sat there for a few minutes in an attempt to clear my head. When I clicked start, the exam began, first with some instructions and then with some sample questions. When I felt myself tensing throughout the exam, I would take a deep breath, bend my fingers back a little, and stretch my neck from side to side. My exam was 117 questions, and it seemed to last forever. When the exam closed, I said a short prayer and exited the testing area.

Our deeprest fear is not that we are inadequate. Our deepest fear is that we are powerful beyond measure. It is our Light, not our Darkness, that most frightens us.
-Marianne Williamson
Reflection: If you weren't afraid of your own power, what would you allow yourself to step into now?

CHAPTER 10-
NIGHTENGALE

Elmore was waiting outside in his car. We parked his car at his cousin's house and took my vehicle to New Jersey. When we got there, I was tired, but I made every effort to be as social as possible. His family reunion was at a hotel in Middlesex County, and it was late when we arrived. Most of the food was already gone, so I settled into a chair with a cup of coffee, daydreaming about sleep. We left two hours later and drove to our hotel to sleep. We were only there for two days, and that was just fine with me. The day we were supposed to leave, Elmore came up with some excuse as to why we needed to stay longer. He said he needed to see a client of his before going back to Virginia. I flat out refused. When he got in the car, I headed for the turnpike, and he was furious. He opened the door of the car while I was driving and threatened to jump out. I was over it and kept driving. He eventually closed the door but wouldn't talk half the way home.

When I called the NCLEX number the next day to see if I had passed the exam, no results were available yet. I needed some good news so I have it a few hours and called back again and I heard a message "Arnita Gray licensed as a Registered Nurse in the state of Virginia with license expiration date of 08/2005". I screamed Oh my God, I passed! It was what I needed to hear. I knew right then that I would be okay regardless. I was going to heal the sick and nurse the broken. I wanted to be a good nurse. Although there was no formal celebration for my achievement, Elmore did take me to dinner. I dove into my internship at the local hospital and began learning all I could about being a prudent nurse and applying evidence-based practice.

A few weeks later, I found two ticket stubs to a concert at the Pavilion on the night Elmore stayed out, claiming to be at the office. All I could think was what kind of man lets the sun rise on him holding a woman other than his wife, who was worried sick waiting for him at home? Is he even a real man? To think that I was cuffed and hauled off to jail for scratching him after he had spent money and time with another woman all night long. To confront him again would have been foolish, so I began preparing for the inevitable.

I transferred from the day shift to the night shift due to the unending drama among the staff. It was anything but what you expected nursing to be. Nurses are known to be supportive, caring, and honest. They say nurses eat their young, and sometimes it's true. They bully each other and compete for the doctors' attention. The new nurses must take the challenging assignments. It was so mind-blowing that I conducted qualitative research on bullying among nurses. The ANA put out a statement that "Incivility, bullying, and violence in the workplace are serious issues in nursing, with incivility and bullying widespread in all settings". Did I choose the wrong career? Not much later, while I was working the night shift at my new job at the hospital, Elmore moved out half the furniture and left not a note the first. He just left me, just like that. For the first time in my life, I felt that this breakup may have been the God's will.

Be thankful for what you have; you'll end up having more. If you concentrate on what you don't have, you will never, ever have enough.
-Oprah Winfrey
Reflection: What is one thing you can appreciate today that you've been overlooking?

CHAPTER 11- DISSENT

There was a very odd sense of peace suddenly. I found myself a good therapist through my health plan at work, and she got me on some antidepressants to help me with the burden of loss and starting over. She employed modalities fitting for my situation, and journaling helped too. I stopped shopping and spending as a coping mechanism. I saved every penny I could for a rainy day. I turned to prayer and family more than I ever had. It's funny how we remember the importance of prayer during a crisis. My faith was renewed, and I found solace in knowing someone other than myself had the final say, and God promised to never leave nor forsake me. I wrote and plaqued my own words of encouragement so I would read them every day, and it read:

In my quietest and most brilliant moment I am thinking "of course I can do rise above this". When you are loving too much, it is ecause you are trying to overcome the old fears, anger, frustration, and pain from childhood, and to quit is to surrender a precious opportunity for finding relief and rectifying the ways you have been wronged. A rule of them is, The more difficult it is to end a relationship that is bad for you, the more elements of the childhood struggle it contains. A woman with a healtheir backgroud has responses and thus relationships that are very different, because struggling and suffering are not so familiar, not so much a part of her history, and therefore not so comfortable.

My First Real Holiday
When we descend into New Jersey for the Christmas holiday, I am almost giddy in anticipating the holidays with family the "right way". There's no man to fight, no ill feelings of any kind, not a care in the world. I feel no shame when having that second slice of pie, or when missing a fake lash the next morning. There is, however, my two children, my mom and step-dad, my old stomping grounds, the chill of the North Wind, and the merriment of the holiday...and I'm still young yet as I look toward the future.

—

My hope is that you come to see how every step of your journey has been guiding you toward your own excellence. May you uncover your magic, your strength, and the deep well of love that lives within you.

I hope you find the golden threads—those quiet truths and hard-won lessons—that help you weave an inner kingdom strong enough to hold the life you choose. And may you share the threads you discover, offering them freely to help other heroines and heroes find their way through their own unfolding paths.

Love and guidance are always with us, steady and enduring, carrying us through the shadows of our hearts and the valleys of our souls. They remind us of our beauty and our light, gently leading the lost pieces of ourselves back home.

You Can Connect with Me at CareByArnita.com.

APPENDIX

QUALITATIVE RESEARCH	
ARTICLE	Wright, W., & Khatri, N. (2015). Bullying among nursing staff: relationship with psychological/behavioral responses of nurses and medical errors. Health Care Management Review, 40(2), 139-147. doi:10.1097/ HMR.0000000000000015
BACKGROUND	The aim is to examine the relationship between bullied nurses with the outcomes including psychological responses and medical errors. The aim is very clear and makes plenty sense. There are psychological, physical, and financial costs associated with bullying. Healthcare organizations need to reduce negative components to allow their nurses to perform at their

	best.
LITERATURE REVIEW	Twenty-four past articles were cited in this article. The research notes "Multiple studies have determined that many health care workplaces possess negative environments that foster disrespectful attitudes, inappropriate behaviors and bullying" (Cleary et al., 2010) Another high note in reviewing her literature is (Macintosh et al. 2010) noted that workplace bullying is 16 times more likely to occur in the healthcare industry versus other sectors. Strong validity given for the researcher's chosen topic. The researcher used several articles that were more than five years old, I would like to have seen some a little more recent.
METHODOLOGY	This is a Level III B Qualitative Grounded Theory research project examining how bullying affects the functioning and psychological state of nurses. Using an internal email system, 1,078 nurses of three facilities at University Hospital System in the Midwest were asked to complete the questionnaire. 248 questionnaires were returned and 241 of that number were usable. The nurses' questionnaire responses were transcribed into a vast amount of data. Grounded theory tools like Rosenstein and O'Daniel's modified scales and the NAQ-R (Negative Acts Questionnaire Revised) were used to measure psychological responses and medical errors.

DATA ANALYSIS	The researcher uses descriptive statistics, particularly frequencies, to analyze data. Conclusion validity is evident here because conclusions about the relationship between nurse bullying and how it affects psychological response and medical duties is reasonable, and the research shows reliability.
CONCLUSION	The researcher concludes that the findings of this research suggest that bullying behaviors exist and affect psychological/ behavioral responses, such as stress and anxiety, and medical errors. I concur with this conclusion speaking as a nurse who was the quiet nurse and sometimes mistaken for a push-over. Stress can lead to med errors, withdrawal, and no confidence. The patient suffers in this type of environment.

Upon assessing the evidence presented in the research, the researcher's conclusion is well supported. The researcher concludes that the findings of this research suggest that bullying behaviors exist and affect psychological/behavioral responses, such as stress and anxiety, and medical errors. Let's start with the article's background; it states that workplace bullying is 16 times more likely to occur in healthcare than any other sector. That's a big deal. It supports the conclusion. When we examine the literature review, we can see that 24 articles were cited on this topic and that multiple studies have determined that many health care workplaces have negative environments with disrespect and bullying. It too supports the conclusion. Providing questionnaires to nursing staff on bullying and how it may have affected their psychological state and functioning is primary research that shapes this conclusion. 241 of the questionnaires were able to be used, and descriptive statistics are used to analyze the data. There is conclusion validity here.

Participants were advised that completion of the survey indicated their consent to participate, and responses would not be identified individually. They were also informed that the data being collected was voluntary and would be confidential. The purpose of the study was reviewed with the Director of Nursing for support and consent to proceed.

One of the biggest limitations in this study is that the questionnaire was distributed via email through nursing managers and supervisors. Surveys may have not been forwarded to staff, especially by managers having bullying tendencies. Participation was a big limitation because out of 1078 nurses only 248 returned the questionnaire. 837 nurses did not participate.

It's been said "nurses eat their young". Nurses must see themselves as being on the same team, and healthcare administration has to mitigate bullying from the workplace. Nurses who witness such behavior must report it immediately and ensure that it does not impede the care of the patient. Leaders of the organization have the primary role to address bullying behaviors. They must lead by example so that their behaviors trickle down and impact organizational culture.

Sources

Cleary M., Hunt G., Horsfall J. (2010). Identifying and addressing bullying in nursing. Mental Health Nursing 31, 331–335.

MacIntosh J., Wuest J., Gray M., Cronkhite M. (2010). Workplace bullying in health care affects the meaning of work. Qualitative Health Research 20 (8), 1128–1141

Wright, W., & Khatri, N. (2015). Bullying among nursing staff: relationships with psychological/behavioral responses of nurses and medical errors. Health Care Management Review, 40(2), 139-147. doi:10.1097/HMR.0000000000000015

Made in the USA
Middletown, DE
28 January 2026

27650146R00038